The Rules for Cats

Other Books by Leigh Anne Jasheway

Bedtime Stories for Cats

Bedtime Stories for Dogs

The Rules for Dogs:
The Secret to Getting Free Treats for Life

Give Me a Break:
For Women Who Have Too Much to Do!

The Rules for Cats

The Secret to Getting Free Catnip for Life

Leigh Anne Jasheway

Andrews and McMeel

A Universal Press Syndicate Company

Kansas City

Library of Congress Cataloging-in-Publication Data
Jasheway, Leigh Anne.
    The rules for cats : the secret to getting free catnip for life /
by Leigh Anne Jasheway.
    p.   cm.
ISBN 0-8362-3291-7 (pbk.)
1. Fein, Ellen. The rules—Parodies, imitations, etc. 2. Cats—
Humor. 3. American wit and humor. I. Title
PN6231.P3J37   1997
818'.5407—dc21

96-51689
CIP

This book is not associated with *The Rules* by Ellen Fein and Sherrie Schneider and is not published by the publisher of *The Rules.*

To Copper, Slate, and Maddy Lou, my dog children who always play with their food and never clean their rooms, but I don't care. And to the eight cats I grew up with who taught me how to scratch and claw until got what I wanted. Finally, to Paul, my husband, the only human who'll put up with me.

Contents

The Rules for Cats

The History of
The Rules for Cats

A long time ago (at least five or six shedding seasons), my mom told me to sit down, she had something to say to me that was very important. So I sat. Well, actually, first I batted around a ball of yarn, then I ran under the bed, then I bolted into the kitchen where I licked the kitchen faucet. Then I sat down. Hey, no kitten worth her catnip ever does what she's told the first time around!

When I finally settled down, Mom passed on to me something her mom had told her, and so on and so on. Actually, it was quite a long and boring story. You know how moms are, so I'll just summarize.

Mom told me about The Rules for Cats. These are the basic principles that, when followed, allow all cats to get the love and adoration they deserve regardless of whether they shred the draperies or use the Persian carpet for a litter box. I myself have never done these things, but then, I am an exceptional cat.

Because we felines are by far the most superior species on the planet, every cat should get the attention that cats like Morris the Cat or Socks the First Cat get— limo service with a scratching post in the backseat, food served out of Waterford crystal, our own TV talk show: Catty Jesse Raphael, Secret Service men who call us by our code name: "Your Highness."

Unfortunately, because most cats don't know the rules, they have to settle for an average lifestyle that is really beneath them. It's embarrassing when you think about it.

Ever since the day my mom shared The Rules for Cats with me, I've followed them to a *t*. Well, maybe just to an *m*. I've got a bit of a rebellious streak in me. Don't want to turn into my mother, if you know what I mean.

As a result of living according to The Rules for Cats, I call the penthouse suite of a six-story kitty condo "home." And I rent out the other five stories for a little spending money. My kitty collars are so expensive they're insured by Lloyds' of London, and occasionally I let my person wear them to fancy soirées, but only if she brings me back paté. I just adore paté. And all I have to do is swat my person just once, nicely, with my claws, and voilá, she appears with fresh catnip.

So after years of sharing The Rules for Cats only with my best friends Tiffany, Amber, and Spot (don't ask!) while pretending to chase a mouse around the yard, I decided it was only fair to write them down so that felines everywhere could share in the good life. Well, actually, I didn't write the rules down. I had my people do it for me. It's true. If you don't believe me, I'll have my people call your people.

What Are
The Rules for Cats?

The purpose of The Rules for Cats is to make your person as obsessed with you as you are with yourself.

If you follow The Rules for Cats, your person will start treating you like the king or queen that you are. Begging you to go ahead and sleep on the pillow, they'll take the foot of the bed where the draft comes in. They'll order you expensive trinkets from Meowmecher Schlemmer. They'll take you on vacations to places like Paris, where you can see just how beautiful you look in a beret.

The most important thing about The Rules for Cats is that you have to follow them all. You can't just follow a few of them and skip the rest. That would be like only half-torturing a mouse. It's just not the same. So here they are. Be forewarned. Your life will never be the same!

Meet a Rules Cat

You've probably met dozens, maybe even hundreds, of cats just like Amber. She's not exceptionally beautiful or exceptionally bright. (Let's be honest here, she still falls for that old plastic mouse routine every time!) In fact, when you come right down to it, she's just your average, flea-bitten tubby tabby cat.

But, unlike other, pedigreed cats—cats with names like Queen Edwina of Roxbury by the Sea—who chase after humans and make themselves available every time anyone says, "Here, kitty, kitty," Amber acts indifferent. Even more indifferent than your average cat. She doesn't look up when a human enters the room (a real no-no). In fact, she usually just turns and heads for the nearest closet where she will happily busy herself with shredding designer clothing or leaving hairballs in Italian pumps.

Amber is a classic example of how far a cat can go if she follows The Rules for Cats. After I shared The Rules with her one day in the little kitty's room, Amber immediately transformed herself. And as a result, her human eventually proposed moving to a fourteen-room mansion in Las Vegas. Now she has fresh catnip growing on the windowsill and the entire desert for her cat box.

While other cats are giving out kisses to every Tomcat, Dick, and Harry and hopping into people's laps willy-nilly, the only lap a cat like Amber sits in is the lap of luxury.

If you ask Amber what her secret is, she'll tell you. She'll tell you to stop purring every time someone reaches down to pet your ears. She'll tell you to quit getting so excited over that ball of aluminum foil. She'll insist that you ignore, neglect, and even mistreat humans.

You may think this is manipulation and deceit at its very worst. And you'd be right. But any cat not up to trickery and conniving is not really worthy to carry the mantle of "feline." Face it, if you prefer honesty, openness, and love, you might as well be a dog.

We all know cats like Amber. They seem to be experts at getting what they want with a flick of their tail or a shake of their whiskers. We can learn from them. This book will show you how.

Rule #1 _____

Be a Feline
Unlike Any Other

You don't have to be rich, beautiful, or even nice to have the world at your paws. And it doesn't matter if you're a purebred or an alley cat. You simply have to have the right cattitude.

You know the cattitude I'm talking about. You walk into a room and people notice. They knock themselves down in hopes that you will deign to let them sit nearby. You raise your nose ever so slightly, and your litter box is cleaned and filled with white sand from the Bahamas.

If you are cattitude-deficient, you may need to enroll in Kitty Charm School, where they'll teach you poise, grace, and how to get your human to serve you dinner while balancing a book on his or her head. Sure, it takes time away from your catnap, but in the long run it'll be worth it.

When you've got cattitude, you are never the groveler. You are always the grovelee. You never appear desperate, even if it's been weeks since someone has rubbed your chin and invited you out for liver treats. You never settle, at least not for less than a nice leather loveseat that you can sharpen your claws on daily.

When out with a human, never let on that you're looking for a committed relationship. For all the person knows, you're only in this for fun and are actually seeing several humans. Leave behind a few telltale signs of your other trysts—chewed up telephone bills, a pair of shoe-laces, the gear knob from a Ferrari.

If you follow Rule #1, you're well on your way to your just rewards. Sit back, relax. Your human is on the way to being hooked (as well as clawed and scratched)!

Rule #2 _____

Don't Speak First

People want desperately for you to speak to them because they know that every meow from your mouth is a jewel to be treasured. But the patient cat is the rewarded cat.

Wait as long as it takes for people to speak to you first. Don't be tempted to jump in, even to say something catty. Let your person start the conversation. Okay, so they do speak in gibberish all the time, always harping on silly things like calling you by name. What's in a name anyway? We'll come when we're good and ready.

Just sit there as your person speaks to you with a patient and understanding look on your face. To keep your superior intellectual mind occupied, you might want to plan your itinerary or alphabetize your play toys. Anything to keep from breaking your poise.

Rule #3 _____

Never Ask a
Person to Dance

Sometimes we cats just gotta dance. We hear an old Cat Stevens tune or anything from the Cowsills, and we just gotta boogey. And face it, we've got style, we've got panache. We're grace in motion.

People, on the other hand, are not. They're klutzes. Admit it. Your person can hardly walk and chew gum at the same time. And how many times do you get stepped on in the course of a day? Eight? Nine?

If for some reason you come into a room and a person is attempting to dance, do not run into the closet and moan loudly because this will humiliate and demean them. And as a result, their self-esteem will be diminished, which may cause them to lose their job. Then how are they going to pay for the lifestyle you so richly deserve?

Rule #4 _____

Stare at People
Until They Back Off

There is an important difference between a glance and a stare. A glance indicates you've noticed that someone besides you is present in the room and that perhaps they deserve attention. This is wrong. Avoid glancing as you would avoid jumping into a cold bath.

A stare, on the other hand, is a simple, straightforward way of letting your person know that you know who's in charge here—you, of course. The longer you hold the stare, the more control you will have over your human. Don't be surprised after a half-hour stare-a-thon to find him preparing you a gourmet, candlelight meal, followed by your favorite nightcap (cream and cream!).

Other forms of eye contact that are also recommended are: The Glare, The Glower, and The Sneer. But use these sparingly—you don't want your human to develop an immunity to your powers.

Rule #5 _____

Don't Meet
a Person Halfway

You should in no way indicate pleasure when a person is in the same room. If they want something, they can just darn well come over to where you're grooming yourself on the couch and present a formal, engraved request.

There are a few exceptions to this rule. You may, for example, meet a person halfway if he or she is carrying a large anchovy pizza. You may also violate the rule if a person happens to be surrounded by paparazzi. Hey, no one deserves fame and fortune more than you do! One word of caution, however, you may find your picture the next morning on *The Feline Enquirer* and wind up having to hire a lawyer.

Rule #6 _____

Don't Call
Your Person

Beside the fact that you don't want to dirty your paws by dialing the phone, especially if you've just had your claws done, you certainly don't want your human to realize that even without opposable thumbs, you are capable of mastering just about any piece of technology in the house.

If that happens, before you know it you'll be finding little notes around the house asking you to call the dry cleaner or start the dishwasher. There's nothing that takes the romance out of the relationship quicker than doing mundane chores. Let's face it, that's why help was invented.

Additionally, if you can't get your message to your human without resorting to the telephone, you need some basic lessons in catmunication. A quick primer:

- *Meow:* I need something.
- *Me-ow:* I need something now.
- *Me-ee-ow:* I need something now, and you should get it for me.
- *Me-ow-ow:* I need something now, and you should get it for me if you know what's good for you.

Rule # 7 _____

Don't Return
Your Person's Calls

Every cat knows instinctively not to respond when called by a human. Even looking ever so briefly toward the offending party is a violation of the Kitty Code of Conduct.

However, it is not enough to just not respond when your person calls. They need to be broken of this nasty habit right off the bat. Try this three-step program for training your person to stop calling you and interrupting your precious nap time:

1. Give them "the look."
2. Give them "the swat."
3. Give them "the hairball," preferably on the pillow.

Rule #8 _____

Always End
Phone Calls First

If you are trying to establish a long-term commitment (where your human is committed to keeping you in the style you deserve, and you are committed to allowing that to happen), the phone can be a rude interruption.

When the phone rings, it means that some other *person* is getting the attention that should be yours—all yours. The best strategy is to chew through the phone cord until it shorts out. If you are dealing with a cordless phone, simply dipping it in the toilet a few hundred times should do the trick. Be sure to dry your paws thoroughly afterward.

Should your human carry a beeper, you must immediately remove the batteries and bury them in your litter box. This works best if you use the nonclumping kind.

Rule #9 _____

Don't Go Dutch on a Date

Get out your Catcyclopedia Britannica. It's okay, I'll wait. Now look up Holland.

See that? It's a picture of a person wearing *wooden shoes!* Do you know what it's like to be in a country where everyone wears wooden shoes and every time they step on your tail you hear a crunching noise? Not a pretty picture, believe me.

So for heaven's sake, don't go Dutch on a date. Go Japanese. They always remove their shoes before they enter a room. Now that's class!

Rule #10 _____

Don't Accept a Trip to the Vet After Wednesday

Every cat knows that veterinarians do their best work early in the week. Once Wednesday rolls around, they're tired and cranky. Do you want your eye job or tummy tuck done by someone who can barely keep his or her eyes open? I think not.

Rule #11 _____

Fill Up Your Time Before Your Person Gets Home

There is nothing that can ruin feline/human relationships faster than letting humans know you miss them when they're not home.

Thus, it is vital that you occupy yourself so that when your human arrives, it is obvious that you have had a busy and fulfilling day and couldn't spare a minute to think about them. Whether you spend your time testing the weave of the fabric on the loveseat or knocking everything off the bookshelves is up to you. If you're a black cat, you may even spend your time crossing people's paths. Hey, we're all different. The important thing is that you keep yourself engaged in stimulating activities all day long.

If you find yourself bored at any time during the day, you may want to consider signing up for courses at your local catmunity college. You can take ceramics, belly dancing, or even Windows for Felines.

Rule # 12 _____

How to Act on Dates 1 through 3

Because first impressions are vital, you may want to consider faking it on the first three dates. Pretend to be interested in what the person has to say. Flick your tail once or twice during the conversation. Groom yourself at the dinner table as if to say you care so much for this person you actually want to look good.

An alternative approach is to play hard to get from the very beginning. Climb up a tree, sit on the roof (make sure it's not hot), or hide under the table. Have your date shove that lobster thermidor under the table so that you can enjoy your meal in peace and privacy. So what if your date never sees you? We'll just call this a blind date.

Either of these approaches will leave your human begging for more. One final word. Never, and I mean never, wear Lee Press-On Claws until you've been seeing a person for at least six months. You don't want to look cheap.

Rule #13 _____

How to Act on Dates 4 through Commitment Time

After the third date, you should begin testing your human for compatibility. Accidentally trail kitty litter across his or her face while asleep. Demand that you get your milk before they eat their Cheerios. Insist that they rub scented massage oil into your pads after a hard day.

This is the only way you will be able to determine just how far your human is willing to go to make sure you get what you need. If he or she balks at any request, put them outside for the evening. Try to ignore them, even if they do scratch at the door and whine.

Rule #14 _____

Always End
the Date First

You are a busy kitty with a full schedule—there's Jazzer-cat, your milk-tasters group, the twelve-step program for catnip-a-holics. There's just too much to do in your day to prolong a date, even if you are having a good time.

Some people, however, are pushy, and may insist on seeing you to your kitty door. In order to get rid of them yet assure that they'll be back for more, try one of these surefire excuses:

- I've got to get up early for a big meeting with the Purina board of directors.
- I'm just getting over a nasty case of feline-fluenza.
- I have to get my teeth cleaned.
- It's that time of the month. (I know it's an old cliché, but it works. Believe me, it works!)

Rule #15 _____

Stop Seeing Someone If He or She Doesn't Buy You a Romantic Gift for Your Birthday or Valentine's Day

Special holidays require special gifts. It is not enough for your person to simply remember the day and present you with something like a flea comb or a half-price coupon to the spay and neuter clinic. In fact, if you receive either of these gifts, you should get a good, catty lawyer and sue for irreconcilable differences.

Appropriate birthday or Valentine's gifts include heart-shaped pillows stuffed with catnip, a brass bed (waterbeds are strongly discouraged) with lace spread, and Rodents and Cream Ice Cream. In fact, you're so special you should get all three.

On the other hand, you are not required to purchase any gifts for any occasion. Your presence is gift enough.

Rule #16 _____

Don't Let Your Human See You in the Litter Box More Than Once or Twice a Week

Can we talk? We're all adults here (even if some of us are busy getting in touch with our inner kitten), and we know that everyone has to visit the litter box from time to time.

But there should be a little mystery in every relationship. And the less your human sees you, uh, indisposed, as it were, the more respect he or she will have for you.

This rule can get a little tricky at times. Let's say you have a visit to make and your human is looking right at the litter box. The best thing to do is to crawl under the bed and take care of your business there. Business accomplished—mystery maintained!

Rule #17 _____

Never Kiss on
the First Date

Let's be blunt. Why would you even want to kiss a person? You never know where those lips have been! If you must express some form of affection during the first date, simply remaining awake during the evening is sufficient.

Rule #18 _____

No Heavy Petting

A little flirting is okay. So is rubbing up against a person's leg once or twice. You can even arch your back sensuously and look them straight in the eye.

But never, ever let the situation evolve into heavy petting. This only increases your chances of Feline Pattern Baldness, not to mention the fact that once you let a person pet you, he or she will always want *more, more, more!*

Rule #19 _____

Rules for Intimacy

Remain aloof. Fake it if you have to.

Rule #20 _____

Don't Let a Person Tell You What to Do

Some people have the audacity to think they should be responsible for decisions in the cat/human household. Of course, this is simply because they have not been properly educated.

If your person attempts to suggest you do certain things, such as, "Hop in the pet carrier," or, "Quit walking across my car with your muddy feet," it is up to you to re-mind them who actually wears the collar in your house-hold.

Follow this twelve-step program:
1. Get them to admit they have a problem.
2. Get them to apologize to you.
3. Get them to bring you gifts.
4–12. Repeat steps 2 and 3.

Rule #21 _____

Never Take a
Shower with a Person

Once they've seen you wet, people lose all respect for you. Sure, they'll deny it, but they also deny that they watch *Baywatch* when no one's looking.

Rule #22 _____

Don't Allow Yourself to Be Dressed Up

Don't wear clothing at any time, even if it's really shiny and makes a fabulous noise when you walk—even if they tell you it's for the swimsuit issue of *Cat Fancy*.

Once you pose in clothes, it will come back to haunt you for the rest of your life, and you will never be able to hold your head up high as you walk into a room full of your peers. Of course, you don't have any peers because you're better than everyone. But you know what I mean.

Rule #23 _____

Don't Expect
a Person to Change

Expecting a person to change is like expecting a dog to think. It's just not going to happen.

This reminds me of an old joke. How many people does it take to change the kitty litter? Give up? Four. One to change the litter, one to praise you, one to brush dust off your paws, and one to hold up the mirror so you can see how beautiful you are.

This brings up the question of what to do to deal with those bad habits that most humans demonstrate—habits such as leaving the cap off the toothpaste, never putting the toilet seat down, blowing their nose into dirty socks. . . . You know the things I'm talking about.

Years of scientific research have shown that the one thing that you can do to impact human behavior is to pounce on the human's face while he or she is still sleeping, claws fully extended. While this may not correct the situation entirely, you will feel so much better. And that's all that really matters.

Rule #24 _____

Don't Sleep
with a Person
Until the Time Is Right

This rule is easy to follow since sleeping occupies nine-tenths of a cat's time. Therefore, the rule is that the time is always right. It is still always good advice to never jump into someone's bed the first time you meet them. If you wake up and the person sharing your pillow calls you "Felix" or "Garfield," when your name is obviously "Sheba, Empress of All Things," you've made a serious relationship error.

When you do decide to share a person's bed, make sure to choose the space that is most comfortable to you regardless of how this affects your person. Very often this spot is right on your person's face. You may want to take care to at least leave your person's nose uncovered so that he or she can breathe. A dead person doesn't usually bring you catnip.

Other tips about sharing a bed:

- If you have difficulty falling asleep, make sure everyone else is up too. You can discuss the relationship or have a late-night snack together.
- When snoozing during the day, be sure to claim the only available patch of sunlight or the spot in front of the heater. After all, you've had a long, hard day fantasizing about what it would be like to live with Bill Gates, and you need your rest.

- When you awaken, make sure that you let your person know. This is best accomplished by either (a) jumping on his or her stomach or (b) standing on his or her chest while clawing and meowing.

Rule #25

Don't Live with a Man If He Doesn't Have a Maid

If your person is a woman, you're more likely to have found someone that can keep the household as neat as you require. If, on the other hand, you choose to move in with a man, he'd better have a live-in maid or at least a twice-weekly cleaning service. If you don't believe me, go check under the bed for dust kitties. See, what did I tell you?

Ask yourself this. If a man can't spot dust under the bed, how will he ever be able to tell when your whiskers need waxing?

To be fair, there are some men who are capable of living up to your exacting housekeeping standards. Jerry Seinfeld comes to mind. However, you may find yourself slightly annoyed with Jerry following right behind you with a dustpan.

A good way to tell if a human's standard of cleanliness will be acceptable is with this simple test. Ask yourself these questions:

1. Is there a neon beer sign on the wall?
2. Does the couch moan when you jump on the cushions?
3. Are there life-forms more intelligent than your human growing in the bathtub?

If the answer to any of these questions is yes, run now and never look back.

Rule #26 _____

Don't Date a
Married Man or Woman

Many people who are married have the crazy idea that they should place the needs of their spouse before your needs. Now you know this is ludicrous and flies in the face of all that is good and right, but what can I say, humans are stupid that way.

What you need is a nice, single person, preferably a divorced, middle-aged woman who works at home and has no hobbies or friends. This will give her plenty of time to attend to your needs. You may, however, want to avoid menopausal women. They're always fiddling with the thermostat, not to mention the fact that they occasionally vacuum in the nude because of hot flashes.

You should also never date people with small children or people with dogs. (They're usually idiots. The people, not the dogs. Well, okay, the dogs, too, but I ramble. . . .)

Rule #27 _____

Keep Them Away
from Your Family

You know how they are—your family. Your sister, the Siamese, always takes men away from you simply by batting her baby blues. Your brother, that unmannered tomcat, brings floozies home every night. Your mother begs for attention by purring at everything, the hussy. Your dad constantly embarrasses you by hunting cockroaches and mounting them over the fireplace.

Save yourself the grief and avoid introducing your human to your feline family. It will save you years in pet therapy.

Now, you may find that your human really wants to meet your family—especially if a holiday is right around the corner, a holiday like Thanksgiving or Christmas or The Day Cats Get the Attention They Deserve.

Do anything you can to wheedle out of this meeting. You might try:

- Slashing the tires.
- Batting the car keys down the disposal.
- Developing a slight limp and a pitiful look. Don't go too far with this one. You want your human to feel sorry for you and stay home with you. You do not want to end up at the vet's.
- Whining (hey, it works for dogs).

Rule #28 _____

Follow The Rules for Cats Even When Your Friends Think It's Nuts

Your friends don't really have a clue about what it takes to wrap a human around their paw. So why should you listen to them? In fact, why are they even your friends? When it comes right down to it, you are so much better than them, they're lucky you let them share your air.

Take my advice—get better friends. No, not the ones on TV who sit around all day drinking cappuccino. (Who in their right mind would ruin a nice saucer of milk by pouring coffee in it?) Find cats who can live up to your demanding, but in no way unreasonable, expectations.

Rule #29 _____

Rules for Obedience School

One rule—don't go. Don't even go near. In fact, go over to the phone book right now and rip out the entire O section. You don't want your human getting any stupid ideas—well, any more than he or she already has.

Remember this—the disobedient cat is the pampered cat.

Rule #30 _____

Dealing
with Rejection

While you are allowed . . . no, encouraged . . . no, make that required to reject humans, you should never accept rejection from them. If you should make the first move (for example, you playfully draw blood from their neck with one quick swat), and you find yourself being yelled at or tossed across the room, you should immediately try one of the following:

- Pee on the comforter. (This is ideal if it is goose down and must be dry cleaned.)
- Invite in all your scuzzy friends from the old neighborhood and trash the place.
- Stay up all night watching infomercials for the Abdominizer at full volume.
- Call the Psychic Cats Hotline and stay on the line until the Visa operator breaks through to say, "Your human's credit limit has been exceeded."

Rule #31 _____

Don't Discuss
The Rules with
Your Therapist
or Your Veterinarian

Your therapist is paid to help you think of reasons to blame your mother for things (like you need help), and your veterinarian is paid to stick things, well, you know where. Why would you bother to talk to them about anything? Especially if you're paying for the time?

Take my advice and only share The Rules for Cats with your worthy feline friends. Well, sure, they're not as worthy as you; don't be silly.

Rule #32 _____

Be Difficult
to Live With

Once your relationship with a human is solid—you're sharing a couch, a bed, and a breakfast cereal—you should concentrate on being as difficult to get along with as possible.

Here are some tips:

- Take every opportunity to swat people's feet, especially early in the morning as they are sleepily walking toward the bathroom.
- Carry on late-night chats with several dozen neighborhood pals.
- Make sure there is always a chew toy somewhere it shouldn't be, such as on the couch, in the refrigerator, or in your person's coffee.
- Every time human guests come over, act like a scaredy cat. Go hide under the bed and make pitiful noises so the guests will think that you are not getting the love and attention you deserve. You never know, one of these guests could be Oprah or Steven Spielberg, and the next thing you know, you could be a star.
- Help yourself to regular snacks from the saltwater aquarium in the living room. Be choosy—only select for your treats the fish that cost more than this month's rent.

- Get up really early and watch *Garfield* at full volume. You might want to wear earplugs because you don't want to hurt your sensitive ears.
- If your human ever leaves on vacation without you and gets someone to "sit" with you, make sure you throw up every time the "sitter" comes in the door. Also refuse to eat and start biting all the fur off your paws. A thousand-dollar vet bill will dampen your human's enthusiasm for going away without you again.

Last, but Not Least, 12 Extra Hints

1. When your human asks you out from under the bed, silently count to five hundred thousand. It will make him or her all the more appreciative of your presence.
2. Do the absolute minimum. Always. Try to do even less.
3. When you're invited out to a cat obedience show and you'd rather go bird watching, dig your claws into the Persian carpet and refuse to budge.
4. When walking down the street, drop hints, ever so slightly, that you'd like to be carried.
5. Be affectionate. Look at yourself in the mirror, and tell yourself what a stunning creature you are.
6. If your human is misbehaving, taking you for granted, or treating you like a dog, remember the old pounce-on-the-face-claws-extended-trick. It works

just as well here. Then quietly sit nearby with an innocent look on your face, as if to say, "Did I wake you?"

7. If you are unsure as to whether this is going to work into a long-term commitment, move on with your life. There are plenty of fish in the sea: tuna, seabass, puffer fish, halibut . . . But for heaven's sake, stay away from the dogfish.

8. Occasionally, your human will say things to irk you such as, "Tomorrow we'll go in to get you fixed." Don't get mad, get the scissors.

9. Don't let him or her know that you're afraid to be home alone without a can opener.

10. Don't get angry if your human takes longer to change your litter box than you would like. If you're following The Rules For Cats, it will get done! If not, a nice present in your human's briefcase will usually do the trick.

11. Don't let your humans get sloppy with their looks. Make sure they get their daily exercise by waiting on you hand and foot.

12. Lie on the newspaper so your human pays attention to you, not to a bunch of stupid stories that don't have anything to do with you.

The Rules-at-a-Glance

Rule 1   Be a Feline Unlike Any Other

Rule 2   Don't Speak First

Rule 3   Never Ask a Person to Dance

Rule 4   Stare at People Until They Back Off

Rule 5   Don't Meet a Person Halfway

Rule 6   Don't Call Your Person

Rule 7   Don't Return Your Person's Calls

Rule 8   Always End Phone Calls First

Rule 9   Don't Go Dutch on a Date

Rule 10   Don't Accept a Trip to the Vet
After Wednesday

Rule 29   Rules for Obedience School

Rule 30   Dealing with Rejection

Rule 31   Don't Discuss The Rules With Your
Therapist or Your Veterinarian

Rule 32   Be Difficult to Live With

Well, those are The Rules for Cats. Now that
you're finished, you may want to groom yourself
and get ready to put these time-tested secrets
into action. Or you may just want to take a catnap. You decide.

About the Author

Leigh Anne Jasheway is a comedy writer and stand-up comic who lives in Eugene, Oregon, with her three giant wiener dogs, her much younger spouse (who is regularly mistaken for a high schooler), and lots of dust. Her hobbies include photography, frisbee golf, and lifting short-legged dogs onto the couch. In her next life, she wants her own bed.